TECHNOLOGY IN ACTION

CAR TECHNOLOGY

Mark Lambert

The Bookwright Press
New York · 1990

Titles in this series

Aircraft Technology

Car Technology

Spacecraft Technology

TV and Video Technology

First published in the
United States in 1990 by
The Bookwright Press
387 Park Avenue South
New York, NY 10016

First published in 1989
Wayland (Publishers) Ltd
61 Western Road, Hove
East Sussex BN3 1JD, England

©Copyright 1989 Wayland (Publishers) Ltd

Edited by Jollands Editions
Designed by Alison Anholt-White

Library of Congress Cataloging-in-Publication Data
Lambert, Mark, *1946-*
    Car technology/by Mark Lambert.
    p.   cm—(Technology in action)
    Includes bibliographical references.
    Summary: Discusses the technology used in cars
today – in engines, in fuels, in production, and in other
areas – and the possibilities for tomorrow.
    ISBN 0-531-18329-7
    1. Automobiles—Juvenile literature. [1. Automobiles.]
I. Title. II. Series.
TL147.L35 1990
629.222—dc20   89—17607
                                                              CIP
                                                              AC

Typeset by Direct Image Photosetting Limited, Sussex, England
Printed in Italy by G. Canale & C.S.p.A., Turin

Front cover The car illustrated is the De Tomaso Pantera, an expensive and unusual sports car for the enthusiast. Photograph by courtesy of Fast Lane magazine.

Note to the reader Driving rules vary from one country to another. As a result, some cars have their steering on the left-hand side and some on the right-hand side. The illustrations in this book reflect these variations.

Contents

Of all the machines that people use, the automobile has probably had the greatest influence upon the development of twentieth-century society. During this century, travel, which in the days of the horse-drawn carriage was slow and difficult, has become rapid and easy. In this change, railroads, airplanes and buses have also played an important part. But the automobile is unique because it has given people a freedom not found in any other form of transportation. Only in a car can people travel swiftly to any destination they choose, at any time they wish. In addition, the car is not merely a means of transportation; it has also become a symbol of status, wealth and fashion. Modern cars vary enormously in design and power. They range from small, economical types to large cars of high performance.

The automobile appeared toward the end of the last century. It developed from the wedding of two technologies. One of these, the horse-drawn carriage, had been in use for hundreds of years. The other was a new invention, known as the internal combustion engine, which had been developed by a number of European pioneers. Among these were two Germans, Gottlieb Daimler and Karl Benz, both of whom began to develop automobiles in the mid-1880s. In 1888 Benz was the first to begin selling cars to the public in Germany, and by 1900 there were manufacturers in France, the United States and Britain.

A modern automobile show (left) is similar to an automobile show of the 1950s (above). The cars, however, have changed greatly. Today's cars are more reliable, more comfortable and many are more economical.

The automobile was developed to replace the horse and carriage, but did not become a popular form of transportation until the 1920s. Since then more and more cars have appeared on the roads, and today the automobile has become an essential form of transportation.

Unfortunately, the benefits of the car are not without cost. The car, if driven carelessly, can be a very dangerous machine, and every year thousands of people are killed in road accidents. The accident figures continue to

Freeway traffic in Sydney, Australia. The automobile is a part of everyday life in all developed countries.

increase, because cars, although a great deal safer than they used to be, are also much faster and there are more of them. Cars also create another problem. Exhaust fumes add greatly to air pollution. Important advances in electronic fuel injection and catalytic converters help to reduce exhaust emissions, but the number of cars continues to increase.

The modern automobile was developed by combining a number of different technologies, such as combustion (fuel-burning), materials and electricity. Each of these technologies contributes toward one or more of the systems that together make up the car as a whole. As scientists and engineers discover more about the science involved in these technologies, improvements are made in the design of the systems. As a result, the performance, efficiency and safety of cars is constantly improved. Car manufacturers go on producing new models as the various technologies change.

The main features of the automobile had all evolved by the year 1900. Basically, a car is a box on wheels. But of course there is a great deal more to it than this. The "box" must have an engine to drive the road wheels and there must be ways of controlling speed and direction when it is moving.

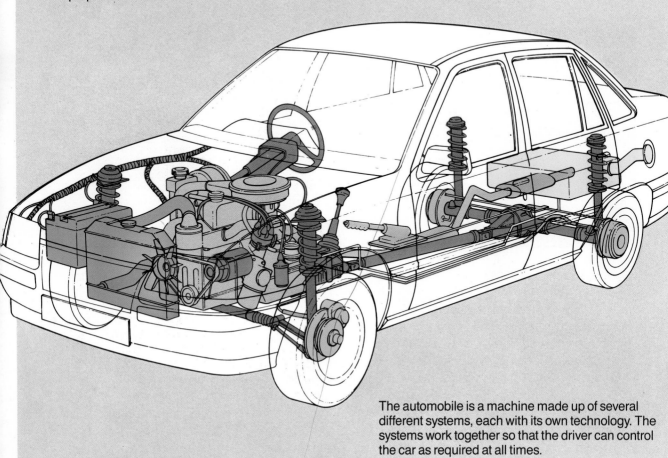

Below The car shown in the illustration is fitted with rear-wheel drive transmission. Power is transmitted to the rear wheels by means of a propeller shaft.

The automobile is a machine made up of several different systems, each with its own technology. The systems work together so that the driver can control the car as required at all times.

Power is provided by the engine. This makes a crankshaft revolve, and the turning movement is then passed to the road wheels by means of a transmission system. The engine speed can be varied, and by using the correct gear, the driver can control the movement of the car at different speeds, backward or forward. A steering system, connected to the front wheels, allows the driver to control direction. When necessary, the driver can slow the car or bring it to a halt by the use of brakes.

There are several other systems. The fuel system supplies gasoline or diesel fuel to the engine. The cooling and lubricating systems prevent the engine from overheating and seizing up. The exhaust system carries away the waste gases produced by combustion and helps to reduce engine noise. The electrical system provides energy for starting the car and, in gasoline engines, produces the sparks needed to ignite the fuel. It also provides power for additional equipment, such as lights, indicators, ventilating fans and radios. The body provides driver and passengers with protection. The suspension system, together with comfortable seating, provides a smooth ride.

Throughout the world there are numerous car manufacturers, all competing against each other to sell as many cars as possible. As a result each car manufacturer employs teams of scientists and designers whose sole job is to improve technologies and develop new models.

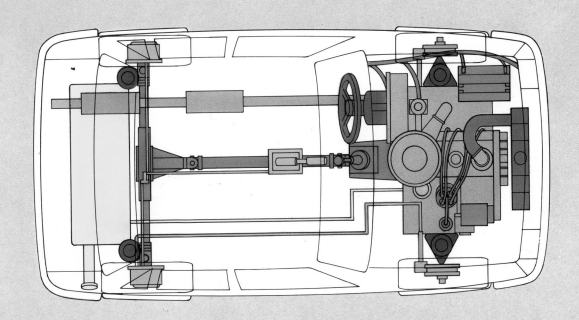

Braking system

Cooling system

Electrical system

Engine

Exhaust system

Fuel system

Steering system

Suspension system

Transmission system

The illustration is a plan view of the car shown on page 6, as though seen from above. It is equipped with left-hand steering, used in most countries of the world. Some countries, including the United Kingdom, have the steering wheel on the right-hand side, and the cars are driven on the left side of the road.

An internal combustion engine takes chemical energy from a fuel and converts it into kinetic energy (the energy caused by motion). A typical gasoline engine has one or two pistons that move up and down inside tight-fitting cylinders. As each piston moves downward, it draws a mixture of air and fuel through one or more inlet valves into the cylinder. The piston then moves upward again to compress the fuel mixture, and a spark ignites the fuel. As the tightly packed gas burns, it expands greatly, forcing the piston downward. This downward movement is converted into rotary movement in a crankshaft connected to the bottom of the piston. The spinning crankshaft then pushes the piston upward again, forcing the burned gases out through one or more exhaust valves. The process is illustrated at the foot of page 9.

The basic design of the automobile engine has altered very little over the years. The cylinders are holes bored into a block of cast iron or aluminum alloy. To keep the metal parts well below their melting point, an engine is cooled either by water circulating in passages in the cylinder block or by air passing over fins on the outside. The internal combustion engine is very inefficient. About forty percent of the energy is lost in the cooling system, and twenty percent vanishes in the form of exhaust. Scientists are constantly trying to solve this problem by research into new materials. In the future some engines may be made of ceramic materials, or even plastics, which can withstand very high temperatures, and will not need cooling.

The most common type of engine in use today is the four-cylinder in-line gasoline engine. Other engines have six or eight cylinders, which may be laid flat or arranged in a V. One type of rotary engine, the Wankel engine, is used in a few cars. This has no pistons or cylinders. Instead, triangular rotors revolve inside a specially shaped casing (see page 34).

The Ford assembly line at the Ford factory, Michigan, in 1913. The engine is being lowered onto the Model T chassis. Engines have changed very little in appearance since that time. But the wheels and chassis are now very different.

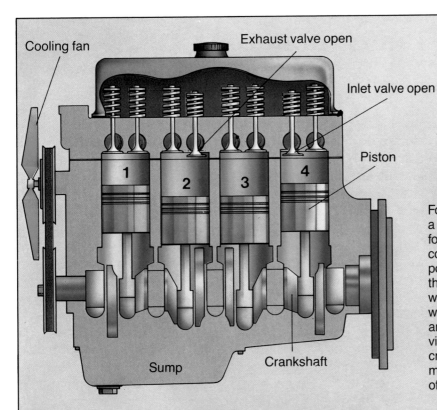

Cooling fan

Exhaust valve open

Inlet valve open

Piston

1 2 3 4

Sump

Crankshaft

For smooth running, the engine of a gasoline-driven car has at least four cylinders. The crankshaft is constructed so as to give the best possible balance as it revolves. If the firing order of the cylinders were to be 1, 2, 3, 4, the balance would be upset and the crankshaft and engine mountings would vibrate. The stress on the crankshaft is reduced to the minimum by having a firing order of 1, 2, 4, 3 or 1, 3, 4, 2.

Below Each cylinder of a car engine operates on a four-stroke cycle, known as the Otto cycle. During the induction stroke, the piston moves down drawing in a mixture of fuel and air through the inlet valve. The valve closes and the piston is forced up again, compressing the mixture. At the start of the power stroke, a spark ignites the fuel, and the expanding gases force the piston down again. Finally the piston comes up again, pushing the waste gases out of the now open exhaust valve.

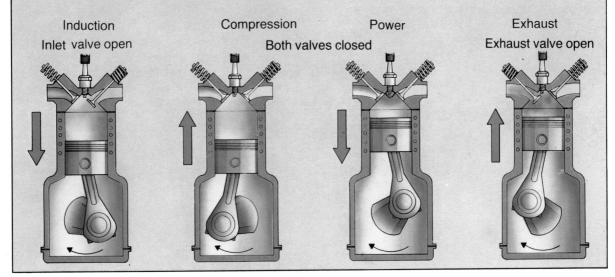

Induction
Inlet valve open

Compression
Both valves closed

Power

Exhaust
Exhaust valve open

In many gasoline-powered cars, fuel is delivered to the engine by means of a fuel pump and a carburetor. In order to burn, gasoline has to be in the form of a vapor gas, and it needs the oxygen in air. The purpose of the carburetor, therefore, is to turn the fuel into a vapor and mix it with exactly the right amount of air. A variety of different types are used, and some cars are equipped with two or more carburetors.

From the carburetor, the fuel mixture passes to the inlet valves of the engine. The vaporized fuel is then ignited by an electrical spark. The current needed for this is produced by the ignition system, which generally consists of an ignition switch, a battery, a coil, a distributor and spark plugs (one to each cylinder). The battery supplies electric current, and the coil and distributor together build up the high voltage needed to produce the spark. The distributor also delivers the high-voltage current to each spark plug in turn. Split-second timing is necessary to ensure that the spark is produced at exactly the right moment. This is achieved by a timing chain, gears or belt, driven by the crankshaft. This in turn, drives a camshaft, which controls the speed of the distributor and the opening and closing of the engine valves.

Not all cars have a carburetor. A number of modern cars use a system known as fuel injection instead. In such cars the fuel pump passes fuel to a fuel distributor. This in turn delivers accurately timed, measured amounts of fuel to injectors, which spray fuel vapor into the engine. The first fuel injection systems were mechanically operated, but many modern cars have electronic fuel injection. Sensors constantly monitor such things as engine temperature, throttle position, ignition timing and the amount of oxygen in the exhaust gases. The task of processing all these different pieces of information in a variety of ways is something that only a microprocessor can achieve.

A normal ignition system has to produce up to 24,000 sparks every minute. However, many modern cars need much higher spark rates, which can be produced only by electronic ignition systems. The whole system is controlled by a microprocessor. Electronic ignition improves performance and fuel consumption, and is much easier to service.

This advanced research engine uses fuel injection, and each cylinder has two inlet valves instead of one. The throttle is controlled by a computer rather than by a direct link to the accelerator pedal.

At the heart of a automobile is the engine. Here all the major mechanical and electrical systems are linked together. The fuel, electrical and cooling systems work together with the engine to produce the power needed to drive the crankshaft.

A spark plug consists of two metal leads separated by a ceramic insulator. At the bottom of the spark plug the leads are separated by a small gap. When a high-voltage current flows down the central lead, a spark jumps across the gap igniting the fuel.

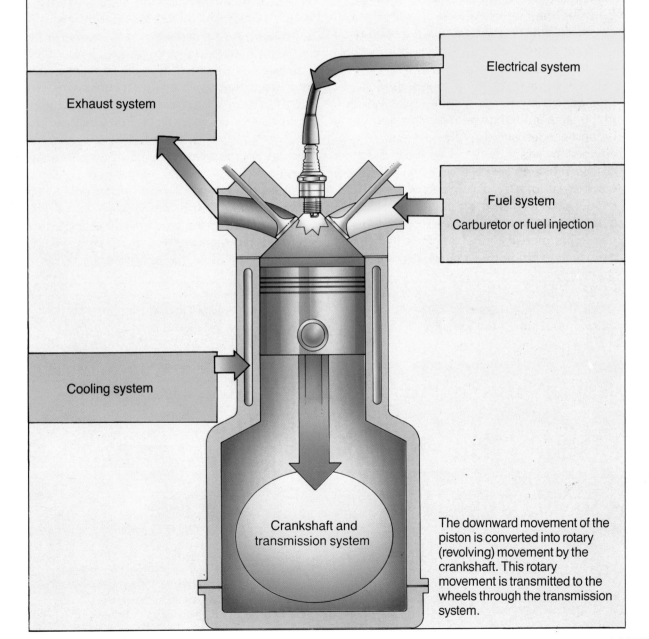

Electrical system

Exhaust system

Fuel system
Carburetor or fuel injection

Cooling system

Crankshaft and transmission system

The downward movement of the piston is converted into rotary (revolving) movement by the crankshaft. This rotary movement is transmitted to the wheels through the transmission system.

11

Economy and pollution

In recent years, fuel economy has become a matter of growing importance since at some time in the future, supplies of crude oil, the source of gasoline and diesel fuel, may run out. However, at present there is no shortage of these fuels, and since there are few alternatives, car manufacturers have tended to concentrate on improving the efficiency of existing kinds of automobiles.

Modern cars use less fuel partly because their bodies are lighter and more streamlined. At the same time, improvements in engine technology have resulted in the development of engines that use less fuel. Generally, the most economical cars are relatively small and have engines with capacities of less than 0.4 gal (1.5 l). More powerful cars have better acceleration and higher top speeds, but they pay for this by using fuel more rapidly. In some of the latest cars with electronic fuel control, it is possible to change, at the touch of a button, from economy running to high performance.

Motor fuel contains hydrocarbons. These are chemicals made of hydrogen and carbon. When such a fuel is burned in air, oxygen should combine with the hydrocarbons to form water and carbon dioxide. However, the combustion process is never perfect, and other chemicals are formed as well. The gases that leave the exhaust system of a car contain carbon monoxide, unburned hydrocarbons and oxides of nitrogen. In older cars, lead may be present. Lead is sometimes added to gasoline to prevent uneven combustion. New U.S. cars use lead-free gas.

These chemicals pollute the atmosphere and damage health. Carbon monoxide is poisonous, and lead is known to affect brain development of children. Nitrogen oxides and unburned hydrocarbons produce poisonous gases.

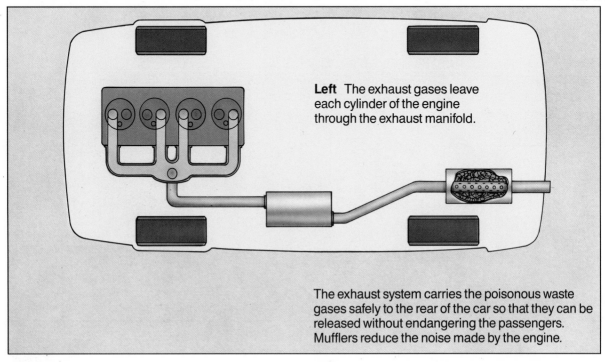

Left The exhaust gases leave each cylinder of the engine through the exhaust manifold.

The exhaust system carries the poisonous waste gases safely to the rear of the car so that they can be released without endangering the passengers. Mufflers reduce the noise made by the engine.

Left A traffic jam in Tokyo, Japan. Tokyo and Los Angeles had severe atmospheric pollution problems caused by fumes from car exhausts. In Tokyo, pedestrians often wore face masks to protect them from the fumes during rush hour periods. All new cars are now fitted with catalytic converters, and the pollution has been reduced as a result.

Attempts are being made to reduce this pollution. Lead-free gasoline makes it possible to use a device called a catalytic converter in the exhaust system. A catalytic converter changes most of these poisons into less harmful substances. Catalytic converters are now fitted to all new cars in the United States and Japan, but European manufacturers favor the use of "lean-burn" engines. These burn fuel more efficiently, but exhaust poisons released in European countries are still five times higher than those permitted in the United States.

Car manufacturers are constantly trying to improve fuel consumption. This strange car, designed by the Ford Motor Company took the world record at the Shell Motor Mileage Marathon in 1984. At a steady pace it completed 3,803 miles on one gallon of fuel.

Driving an automobile requires a great deal of concentration, and can lead to fatigue and stress. The designers of modern cars are paying more attention to reducing these problems to a minimum.

The comfort of the driver is very important. It depends greatly on the shape and position of the driving seat and the position and size of the steering wheel. The driving seat must be adjustable to suit all drivers. The driver should have a clear view of the instruments and be able to operate all the controls with the least amount of effort and fatigue.

The steering wheel operates a series of mechanical linkages connected to the front wheels. Gearing helps to reduce the effort needed to steer a car, and some large cars have power steering. In this, steering is aided by a hydraulic pump driven by the engine.

The driver controls the engine speed by means of a foot pedal linked to the throttle, a movable valve in the air intake of the engine. The power that the engine delivers to the wheels is controlled by means of a gear lever linked to a system of gears in a gearbox. The gears reduce the speed of rotation and increase the turning power of the engine. Different gears are needed, depending on the speed of the road wheels in relation to the speed of the engine. Most cars have four forward gears and a reverse gear. However, many modern cars also have a fifth forward gear, or even a sixth.

In most cars, the driver selects each gear by means of a gear lever. In order to do this, the

The cockpit of this concept car shows a number of features designed to improve comfort and safety. The adjustable, well-padded seats enable the driver to find the most comfortable position. The steering column and the instrument panel can be tilted forward or backward as a single unit, so that it can be adjusted to suit any driver.

gears are disconnected from the engine by means of a clutch, operated by another foot pedal. In other cars, however, the workload of the driver is reduced by having an automatic gearbox, in which the changing of gears is controlled by the speed of the car and the position of the throttle.

From the gearbox, power is transmitted to the wheels via a final drive. In a front-wheel-drive car the engine, clutch, gearbox and final drive form a single unit, and power passes to the wheels via two half shafts. In a rear-wheel-drive car, the final drive is near the rear of the car and is linked to the gearbox by a propeller shaft.

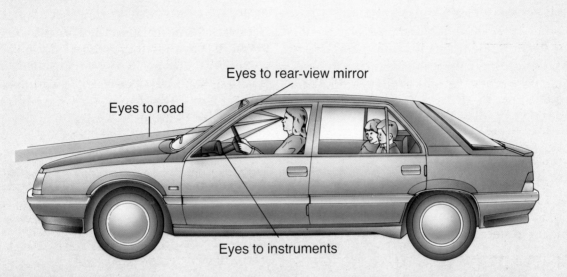

Eyes to rear-view mirror

Eyes to road

Eyes to instruments

Above Driving a car requires a great deal of concentration.The driver has to watch the road ahead and see what might be going to happen. Rear view mirrors must be used frequently to check what is going on behind. The driver should also look at the instruments from time to time. Many things can distract a driver, such as sudden loud noises from passengers in the rear.

Hands on steering wheel, gear lever, and handbrake

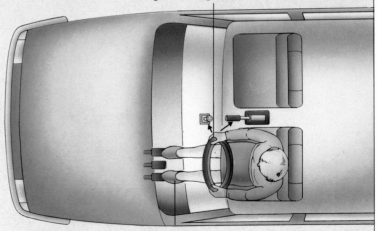

Feet on pedals

A driver controls a car by means of the gear lever, steering wheel and three foot pedals. The right pedal controls the throttle, the middle pedal controls the brakes, and the left pedal operates the clutch. The hand brake is used to hold the car when stationary.

A third foot pedal is used to operate another vitally important system – the brakes. Pressure on the brake pedal is transmitted to a hydraulic fluid contained in a system of pipes and cylinders. The system multiplies the pressure so that a small amount of pressure on the pedal results in a much larger pressure at the brakes. In some cars the braking effort is assisted by air pressure in a servo mechanism powered by the engine. Many of today's cars have drum brakes on the rear wheels and disk brakes at the front. For safety, modern cars have two-part braking systems. If one part of the system develops a fault the other system continues to work satisfactorily. There are several different types of split circuit braking systems.

The tires of a car provide the only contact with the road. Ideally, a tire must be strong enough to withstand damage and yet flexible enough to smooth out road shocks. The early solid rubber tires lacked flexibility, and to solve the problem John Boyd Dunlop, a Scotsman, invented the pneumatic, or inflatable tire. This consisted of a hard rubber casing, enclosing a rubber tube that could be inflated with air under pressure. Since air can be squashed, a pneumatic tire, when inflated to the correct pressure, provides the required flexibility to absorb road shocks. The outer casing of the tire is strengthened by layers, or plies, of over-lapping fibers. These are usually made of very strong nylon or polyester.

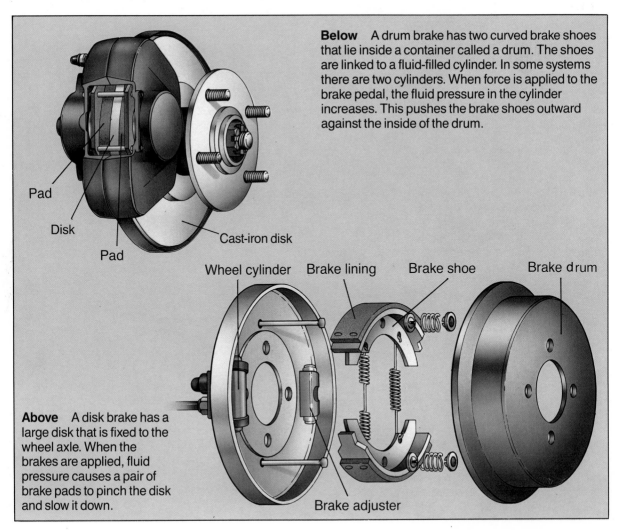

Below   A drum brake has two curved brake shoes that lie inside a container called a drum. The shoes are linked to a fluid-filled cylinder. In some systems there are two cylinders. When force is applied to the brake pedal, the fluid pressure in the cylinder increases. This pushes the brake shoes outward against the inside of the drum.

Pad

Disk

Pad

Cast-iron disk

Wheel cylinder   Brake lining   Brake shoe   Brake drum

Above   A disk brake has a large disk that is fixed to the wheel axle. When the brakes are applied, fluid pressure causes a pair of brake pads to pinch the disk and slow it down.

Brake adjuster

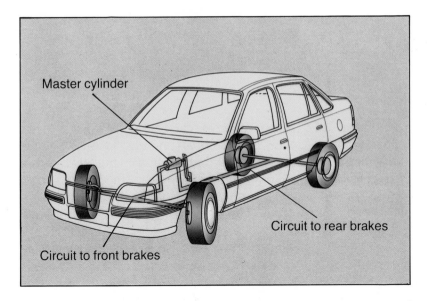

Master cylinder

Circuit to rear brakes

Circuit to front brakes

A dual braking system ensures that if one of the brake pipes develops a leak, part of the system continues to work properly. In the simplest form of dual system, one brake pipe leads to the front brakes, and a separate pipe leads to the rear brakes. A specially designed master cylinder ensures that if one half of the system fails, it is immediately cut off from the other half.

Most modern tires are tubeless. The compressed air is held in by a soft rubber lining on the inside of the tire. The outer layer of a tire is made of a thicker layer of hard rubber. The tread, the part that makes contact with the road, contains deep drainage channels, which prevent water from building up between the tire and the road surface. Adequate drainage channels are vitally important to safe driving in wet conditions. A worn tread may cause a car to skid out of control. In most countries it is illegal to drive a car that has worn tires.

A tire flexes as it rolls along the road, and this flexing uses up some of the energy produced by the engine. In some of the most recently developed tires, new designs and materials have helped to reduce this energy loss. Recently the tire manufacturing company Dunlop has developed a safety tire that can be used safely for up to 100 mph (160 km) after being punctured.

The brake pipes are visible on this old Aston Martin at Brooklands, England, 1934.

The body of a modern car is designed to carry people comfortably and safely. It is attached to the wheel axles, or in some cases a base-frame called the chassis, by means of a suspension system that keeps the passengers from being jolted by bumps in the road.

Early cars were built in two parts, a chassis and a body. In most modern cars, the chassis and body are combined. Sheet steel is cut and pressed into shaped panels. Where necessary, strength and rigidity are provided by ribs, welded box sections and extra thicknesses of steel. The panels are then welded together to produce the finished shell. Some European cars have one or two partial chassis frames, or subframes, making assembly and repair easier.

Most modern cars are constructed from steel, which is cheap and easy to use. Its main disadvantage is that it rusts very quickly, but this problem can be partly overcome by the use of special paints, underbody sealing compounds and electrochemical treatment. Sometimes aluminum is used instead of steel, but it is more expensive and less rigid. Glass-reinforced plastics, which do not rust at all, are also used, but they are weaker and require the use of a separate steel chassis. In the future, other plastics may be used, such as the tough plastics already used to make such parts as bumpers. At present, the strong modern composite materials based on carbon fibers are usually too expensive to use in cars.

In the early 1900s driving was very uncomfortable.

The purpose of the suspension system is to absorb the energy contained in shocks from the road. In early cars this energy was taken up by leaf-springs, but in modern cars coil springs or torsion (twisting) bars are more commonly used. Left to itself, a spring would continue to bounce for some time, resulting in an uncomfortable ride. So the suspension system also includes fluid-filled shock absorbers that absorb some of the energy from the springs.

Since many roads have an uneven surface, most cars now have independent suspension, in which each of the wheels moves up and down independently of the others. There are a variety of designs. Among the most common forms of suspension are the MacPherson strut and the double wishbone. In some cars, the springs and shock absorbers are replaced by fluid-filled or gas-filled units. The gas used in the latter system is normally nitrogen.

For many years, designers have used humans to provide information on seat comfort. Now computer dummies can be used to measure seat comfort.

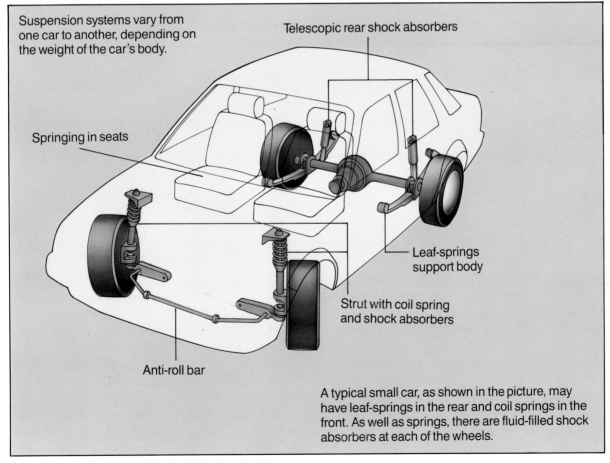

Suspension systems vary from one car to another, depending on the weight of the car's body.

Telescopic rear shock absorbers

Springing in seats

Leaf-springs support body

Strut with coil spring and shock absorbers

Anti-roll bar

A typical small car, as shown in the picture, may have leaf-springs in the rear and coil springs in the front. As well as springs, there are fluid-filled shock absorbers at each of the wheels.

A new car design is tested to see what will happen in the event of a crash. An inflatable bag, designed to protect the driver, is also being tested.

Safety has become an important factor in the design of modern cars. The body has to provide the driver and passengers with as much protection as possible in a crash. The safest cars are those in which the occupants sit in a strong rigid case. In the event of a head-on crash, the engine and gearbox are pushed safely underneath the cage. At the same time, the front body section crumples on impact and absorbs a large part of the shock. The rear section is also designed to crumple. Many cars now have bumpers mounted on shock absorbers.

The doors and side panels have to be strong enough to resist impact from the side, and the doors should neither jam shut nor spring open in a crash. It is impossible to see through a safety glass windshield that has just been "crazed" or "starred" by impact with a stone. But modern laminated glass has a tough plastic film between two sheets of glass. So windshields made of laminated glass do not shatter, and visibility remains good.

Inside the modern car there are a number of safety devices. Seat belts, on both the front and rear seats, are vital. In a head-on crash, anyone not wearing a seat belt is likely to be thrown forward through the windshield or onto the seat in front. A well-padded interior softens any impact for the occupants. Padded headrests prevent neck injuries if the occupants are thrown back into their seats. A collapsible steering wheel helps to prevent injury to the driver in the event of a minor collision.

Attention is also being paid to the safety of other, even more vulnerable, road users, such as cyclists and pedestrians. Outside rear-view mirrors can be made to give way under impact. Injuries can also be reduced by ensuring that a pedestrian is directed over rather than underneath the car. A hood made of soft sheet metal helps to cushion the impact.

New car designs and crash protection equipment have to be tested. Computers can be made to simulate crashes, but the most certain method of testing a new design is to stage crashes under realistic conditions. Test cars are filled with measuring equipment, and the crash is recorded on high-speed film. Very realistic dummies are used to assess the effects of a crash on the occupants of the car.

Most countries now have laws that are designed to protect drivers and their passengers, and all other road users. These include the fitting and use of safety belts for all passengers.

In highway accidents, a head-on collision is likely to cause the most damage to the car and its occupants. In this road safety test, high-speed cameras are being used to monitor what happens to the car's soft spots at the moment of impact.

Right A dummy driver seated in the same vehicle before the test.

Driving a car is something that many people do every day, without needing to think about it very much. After some years of practice the movements and reactions involved become almost instinctive. However, driving an automobile well requires skill and training. Good driving also requires a considerable amount of thought. Ignorance and lack of attention make for bad driving habits and carelessness, and these often result in accidents.

Good driving helps to reduce the cost of motoring. Rapid acceleration and high-speed driving use up a great deal of fuel. Accelerating more slowly and driving at more moderate speeds not only keep down fuel consumption but also reduce wear on moving parts. Such things as engines, brakes and tires last longer before they have to be repaired or replaced.

More important, good driving saves lives; most accidents are caused by careless driving. Modern cars are capable of high speeds, and many accidents are the result of driving too fast. In most countries there are speed restrictions, but drivers often ignore them. Even speed limits are not always a good guide. Safe driving speeds depend a great deal on road conditions, and cars should always be driven more slowly in wet or icy conditions .

In drag racing, cars accelerate from the starting line so rapidly that the wheels spin. The heat generated causes the tires to burn, and the tread is very quickly worn away. It would be bad driving and costly to do this with a normal car.

An aerial view of a bend on an expressway in England shows the aftermath of a pile-up. This involved 120 vehicles, and the pile-up happened in thick fog. The police reported that most of the cars had been traveling too fast and too close to each other at the time of the accident.

Safe driving depends on the driver's being alert and in full control of the car. The driver must be aware of other road users at all times. Turning, cornering, overtaking and reversing must be carried out carefully, using warning signals when necessary. The greatest concentration is needed when driving at night, in heavy traffic and in difficult conditions, such as fog or snow. Highway driving needs special care, as it is very easy to become drowsy or lacking in attention when cruising at a constant high speed. Accidents on highways are often caused by driving too close to the car in front. This is particularly dangerous when there are patches of fog or when the road surface is icy.

Fatigue is another cause of accidents. Although car designers are trying to help reduce this problem, in the end it is the responsibility of drivers to ensure that they do not drive when they are tired. Fatigue impairs judgement and reduces the time taken to react in an emergency. Alcohol and many kinds of drugs have the same effect, and in many countries there are laws against driving with alcohol in the body. The safest rule is not to drive at all after drinking alcohol.

In the early days of automobiles, cars were expensive luxuries and only the rich could afford them. Today, luxury cars are still built, often individually in small numbers. Names such as Rolls Royce, Mercedes Benz and Cadillac are associated with luxury cars, which remain expensive and are aimed at a small number of people at the top end of the market.

Most of today's cars, however, are produced for what is called the mass market. Cars first became more widely available in 1908, when Henry Ford began mass-producing the Model T Ford in the United States. After World War I Europeans, too, began demanding cheap mass-produced cars, and competition between manufacturers has been keen ever since. Over the years many companies have appeared, only to disappear again after a short time as the demand for their particular make of car has declined. Others have merged with, or been taken over by, larger firms. Most of today's major car manufacturers are huge companies with production plants and sales organizations in many parts of the world.

The Ford Company's range of Sierra and Sapphire cars includes many body styles.

Luxury cars are expensive to buy and costly to run. At the top of the range are famous makes such as Cadillac (United States), Rolls Royce (Britain) and Mercedes Benz (W. Germany). Fifty years ago there were many more manufacturers making luxury cars than there are today.

The mass market is made up of an enormous range of potential buyers, each of whom may have slightly different needs or preferences. People buy family cars, sports cars, cars for business, and cars for commuting to work – to name just a few. It is difficult for manufacturers to decide how many different models to produce. On the one hand, people have varying tastes, and car buyers like to choose from a wide variety. On the other hand, producing a wide range of individually designed cars slows down manufacture and can be very expensive.

Car manufacturers solve this problem by concentrating on a few basic models, each of which can be varied slightly without affecting mass production. The range of cars based on a single model could include a four-door sedan, a three-door hatchback and a five-door hatchback. Each of these could be produced in three different engine sizes and eight different colors. Simple multiplication shows that the buyer, in this case, has 72 variations to choose from. It is for this reason that there is such a variety of cars to be seen.

Further variations are created by the use of additional or optional equipment. This may include such "extras" as a sun roof, electrically operated windows, central locking and audio system. On many models such fittings are standard equipment. Generally, cars nearer the luxury end of the market have the largest number of these refinements.

A new car begins its life on a designer's drawing board. The designer begins with a concept, or idea, that outlines the basic type of car that is to be designed. The concept includes such things as the approximate size of the car, the number of passengers, the type of body (sedan, hatchback or station wagon) and the layout of the engine, transmission and suspension. Detailed full-size drawings are made to help marketing experts decide whether or not the new car will appeal to the buying public.

During the next stage, skilled modelers build up a full-sized clay model on a frame made of wood and plastic. Several models may be made to show different style ideas.

The finished model can now be scanned electronically and the design passed to a CAD (computer-aided design) station. The computer

Car designers use computer-aided design (CAD) to help them create new models.

is used to analyze how all the various parts of the car are likely to behave in use and to help make suitable changes in their design. Detailed drawings can be produced on a plotter and in some cases the final specifications can be transferred directly to computer-controlled machines used in manufacturing the parts.

One of the major design considerations in the modern car is streamlining to reduce air resistance. Air resistance is measured using a wind tunnel and a clay model of the car, which may be anything from one-fifth scale to full size. The measurement used to assess the car's air resistance is known as the drag factor. The overall shape of the car is important in reducing drag. Generally, the most streamlined cars have the lowest drag factors. Curved surfaces produce less drag than sharp corners, and fittings, such as outside rear-view mirrors, mud flaps and roof racks, should ideally be kept to a minimum. Other factors such as weight distribution and the need for adequate space inside make it impossible to produce a perfectly streamlined car. Nevertheless, improvements are constantly being made. In 1980 the average drag factor was about 0.45, but most of today's cars have drag factors of between 0.30 and 0.40.

Final testing of prototypes takes place on the manufacturer's proving track and in the laboratory, where years of "use" can be condensed into a short space of time. Every part of the new car is thoroughly tested and the cost of servicing and maintaining the car is carefully analyzed. By the time the new model reaches the production stage, vast sums of money have been spent on development.

Left Inside a car design studio. At the back of the room, work is being done on full-scale drawings. Wooden models show possible cockpit designs.

Below A new design being tested in a wind tunnel to show how the streamlining works at different speeds. Computer readings appear on a screen showing the drag factor.

The first motor cars were built by hand. Each car was assembled in one place, and the necessary parts were brought from different parts of the factory. However, in 1908 Henry Ford began producing Model T Fords using a rather different system. Instead of having assembly workers move around the factory, the cars were moved from one assembly point to the next along a production line. The workers at each assembly point had a particular task, which they repeated over and over again as the cars passed. This system is known as mass production and is the same system used by modern car manufacturers.

Henry Ford did not invent mass production. This system can be used to manufacture anything that has to be produced in large quantities, and by 1900 some of the essential ideas of mass production were already in use. In 1798 the American inventor Eli Whitney had pioneered the idea of mass producing muskets using identical component parts. In 1808 the English engineer Sir Marc Isambard Brunel had developed the first production line—a line of precision machine tools for the manufacture of pulleys for sailing ships. Henry Ford combined these ideas with the use of a conveyor belt to produce the moving production line. Within a few years every part of the Model T Ford was being assembled on its own production line and each line was carefully timed to feed a final assembly line at exactly the right speed.

The modern automobile is assembled from thousands of different parts. Nearly all of these are assembled by mass production methods, but not usually in the same factory as the finished car. Many are supplied by completely separate manufacturers. Even the engines are often assembled in separate factories, and international motor companies may have assembly plants in several different countries.

Another feature of the modern automobile production line is that in many factories there are very few human workers. Henry Ford's machines had human operators, but today automatic machines are used in the construction of parts such as engine blocks, wheels and body panels. On the assembly line computer-controlled robots have taken over some of the most difficult and unpleasant tasks, such as welding body panels together and spraying paint. The production line, together with all its feeder lines, is controlled by a central computer.

Above The technique for mass-producing cars originally worked out by Henry Ford is still in use today. But in many factories, robots have taken over the tasks once performed by human workers. This shows Mercedes-Benz cars being assembled.

Left The main assembly line used for building Model T Fords in 1915. This line was supplied with parts from carefully timed feeder lines. At one time a new car rolled off the line every ten seconds.

In the early days of motoring, only the most expensive automobiles could be considered comfortable. Most people traveled in cars for fun, and part of the excitement of driving came from traveling fast in an open-topped vehicle. Within a short time manufacturers were producing a new type of car, the sports car, specially designed for this type of driving.

Sports cars have remained popular ever since. The typical modern high-performance car has a relatively large engine, with a capacity of between 0.5 to 1.32 gal (2 and 5 l). A multivalve engine, in which each cylinder has several inlet and exhaust valves, helps to improve the fuel combustion and increase the power output. Aluminum alloys are often used to reduce the weight of the engine and car body, and the most recent cars have the latest electronic fuel and ignition equipment. Front and rear spoilers are sometimes used to hold a car down onto the road, and four-wheel drive is becoming more common. All these features, which are designed to improve performance, are increasingly being found on less expensive cars.

Sports cars like this 1907 Spyker appeared early in automobile history.

Many sports cars use a supercharger or turbocharger to increase the power output of the engine. Both of these work by forcing extra air into the engine, allowing more fuel to be burned during each combustion stroke. A supercharger is a compressor that is mechanically driven by the engine itself, usually from the crankshaft. A turbocharger is driven by exhaust gases. A supercharger produces boost at all engine speeds, but it actually uses up some of the energy in the crankshaft and at high engine speeds produces less boost than a turbocharger. On the other hand, a turbocharger produces very little boost at low engine speeds. Some rally cars are equipped with both superchargers and turbochargers.

The sports car is designed for performance and speed. However, throughout nearly all of the history of the automobile, most countries have imposed speed limits. Such limits are generally well below the top speeds of most cars, particularly high-performance sports cars. Some modern sports cars can reach speeds of over 140 mph (230 kph), whereas in most countries there are open road speed limits of around 70 mph (110 kph) or even less.

Above   An 8-cylinder engine as fitted to a Porsche Model 928.

Below   This Porsche Model 959 is a four-wheel-drive car with a rear spoiler. This model was originally designed for racing and rally-driving.

13 Racing

As cars in the early 1900s became faster and faster, it was invevitable that people would begin to race them against each other. This had several benefits. Racing provided people with an exciting sport, both to watch and to take part in, and this served to interest people in cars and car design. The race track became a testing ground for cars. In order to race at high speeds, all the different parts of a car had to work much harder than in ordinary road cars. If any part was weak or poorly designed, racing soon made it obvious, particularly so in the case of long-distance races.

Competition was keen on the race track, and there was a constant need to make cars perform better. In order to achieve this, racing car designers worked hard to improve car design. Many components that later became standard on all cars began life on the race track. For example, four-wheel braking and four-wheel drive were both first introduced in racing cars. Radial tires were first used on the race track for better road holding. Fuel injection systems, originally developed to enable aircraft to fly upside down, were also used in racing cars before road cars.

The 1920s and 1930s are sometimes described as the golden age of car racing. This photograph shows a race in 1937, taking place at Brooklands, which was the most popular racing track in England at the time.

Over the years racing cars have become less like road cars. Modern racing cars are divided into different classes, or formulas, each of which is governed by strict rules that specify such things as engine size, engine speed and fuel. The rules are altered from time to time. At present, cars in the top class, known as Formula One or Grand Prix cars, are limited to an engine size of 1 gallon (3½ l). The typical Formula One racing car is a low-bodied, rear-engined vehicle, with a hard suspension, widely spaced wheels, wide tires and spoilers at both front and rear. The body and chassis are built as a one-piece shell, using carbon-fiber composite materials. The engine is controlled by an electronic management system (see page 39), linked to a digital display in the cockpit.

Sports cars are also used for racing, both on race tracks and on ordinary roads. The Le Mans 24-hour race is designed to test the endurance of such cars. Other production cars are also raced in rallies and in stock car races.

Right This 8-cylinder, turbo-charged V-engine was used in the Marlboro McLaren Formula 1 cars that won the 1984 and 1985 World Championships.

Below A Formula 1 Alfa Romeo racing car.

The four-stroke, gasoline-driven piston engine has now been in use for over 100 years during which time it has remained supreme as a power source for cars. Other types of engines have been suggested, but none of them have seriously challenged the piston engine.

External combustion has been tried, in the form of the steam engine and the Stirling "hot air" engine. In a steam engine, fuel is burned outside the engine to generate steam pressure inside. However, such an engine is bulky and complicated to operate and few steam cars were ever built. In the Stirling engine, burning a gas heats up air, which is then cooled again. In the process the air expands and then contracts, causing a piston to move back and forth. The Stirling engine is quiet, efficient and clean. It was invented in 1816, but then ignored for many years, mostly because of construction problems. Recently, engineers have become more interested in this engine.

Another group of engines that have long interested engineers are rotary engines. Such engines produce rotary movement in a crank-shaft directly, rather than indirectly, from the back and forth movement of pistons. However, rotary engines have yet to be widely used in cars except for Mazda sports cars. Wankel engines are very promising, but have so far proved to be rather expensive to produce and operate.

The most successful "alternative engines" are fairly conventional piston engines. One of these

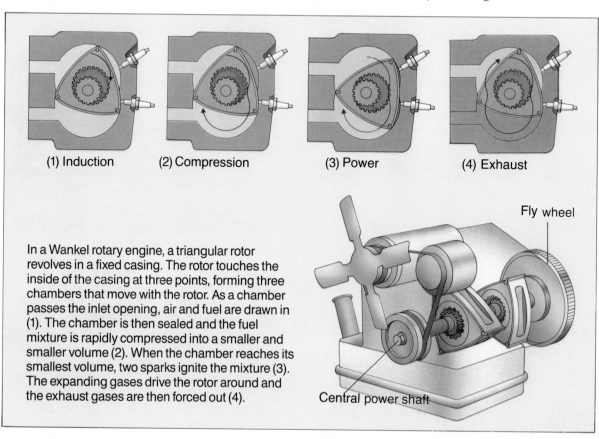

(1) Induction   (2) Compression   (3) Power   (4) Exhaust

Fly wheel

In a Wankel rotary engine, a triangular rotor revolves in a fixed casing. The rotor touches the inside of the casing at three points, forming three chambers that move with the rotor. As a chamber passes the inlet opening, air and fuel are drawn in (1). The chamber is then sealed and the fuel mixture is rapidly compressed into a smaller and smaller volume (2). When the chamber reaches its smallest volume, two sparks ignite the mixture (3). The expanding gases drive the rotor around and the exhaust gases are then forced out (4).

Central power shaft

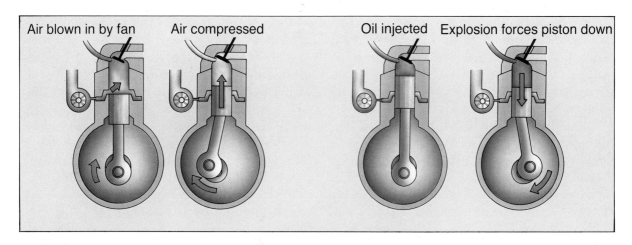

Air blown in by fan | Air compressed | Oil injected | Explosion forces piston down

Diesel engines and gasoline engines are alike in many ways. Diesel engines do not need a spark to ignite the fuel. On the compression stroke the air gets very hot. Then oil is sprayed onto the hot air and the mixture explodes.

is the recently developed stratified charge engine, which is basically a more efficient variation of the gasoline engine. The other is the diesel engine, which has always been more fuel-efficient than a gasoline engine. Until recently diesel engines have tended to be noisy and rather slow, but the latest diesel engines can match the quietness and performance of gasoline engines, and the fuel is slightly cheaper.

However, all these engines are designed to use fuels that are derived from crude oil. The world's oil reserves are being used up at a tremendous rate, and many people therefore believe that the most pressing need is the development of power sources that do not rely on oil. Sooner or later the world's oil reserves will start to dwindle. As they do so, oil will become more and more expensive.

One way of avoiding the need for fossil fuels is to use electricity directly from solar cells. But solar-powered cars do not work without storage batteries unless the sun is shining.

The General Motors solar car, *Sunraycer*, which won the solar marathon in Australia in 1988. When sun shines on the silicon cells, an electric current is produced. Some of this is stored in a battery, which can be used in an emergency to run the car.

The obvious solution to the problem of fossil fuels is to find new fuels. At present, the main alternative to gasoline is ethyl alcohol, or ethanol. This can be created by fermenting sugars contained in plant materials, such as sugarcane and sorghum. Ethanol can be used by itself or mixed with lead-free gasoline to make gasohol. Both ethanol and gasohol are widely used in Brazil, where large areas of land are available for growing fuel crops. Another alcohol that could be used is methyl alcohol, or methanol. It is possible to produce methanol from waste materials, such as industrial and domestic refuse and wood waste from forestry work.

One of the advantages of using alcohols is that they produce much less pollution. Other possible fuels with the same advantage include the gases propane and methane. However, as with gasoline, the combustion of all these fuels still produces carbon dioxide. It is widely believed that increasing amounts of carbon dioxide in the air are causing the earth's atmosphere to warm up by a process known as the "greenhouse effect." Hydrogen gas, on the other hand, produces only water when it is burned, and would thus be an ideal fuel for future cars. But a cheap way of producing hydrogen is needed, and this has yet to be found.

Heat from the sun warms the earth. The heat given off by the earth warms the atmosphere, and some escapes into space. But some of this escaping heat is trapped by fossil fuel gases, so the earth's atmosphere is gradually warming up.

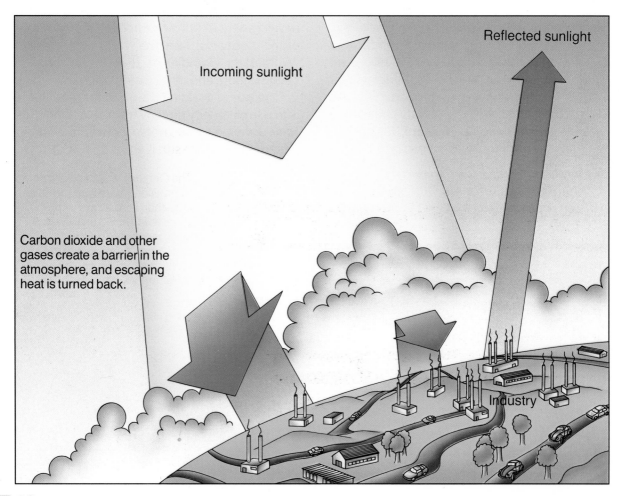

Incoming sunlight

Reflected sunlight

Carbon dioxide and other gases create a barrier in the atmosphere, and escaping heat is turned back.

Industry

Above In Amsterdam, visitors and shoppers can hire electric cars and drive them around the city. For short distances electric cars are a clean and quiet means of transportation. The small electric car seen below is made in France.

The ultimate clean, quiet vehicle is the electric car. Scientists have been trying to develop an efficient battery electric vehicle since the early 1900s, but so far without success. The main problem has always been the great weight of the batteries needed to store the electricity and the need to recharge the batteries every 30 miles (45 km) or so. In some countries electric vans are used for door-to-door deliveries of milk and mail, but as yet no manufacturer has designed an electric car capable of long-distance travel.

Electronic monitoring and control is rapidly becoming an important feature of the modern automobile. This is partly because of the constant need to improve safety and efficiency. Electronically operated devices can generally achieve much faster and more accurate control than purely mechanical devices. At the same time, manufacturers competing for sales need to present their cars as being at the forefront of modern technology. So computers and electronic control systems are among the many refinements featured on the latest cars.

Some of these refinements add to convenience and comfort. Central locking, for example, enables all the doors of a car to be controlled from just one lock, using an electronic "key." Electronically controlled outside rear-view mirrors and seat adjusters are also fitted to some of the latest cars.

More important, however, are the electronic sensors located in the working parts of the car. These monitor useful information, such as fuel level, oil pressure, engine temperature, engine speed, road speed, brake-pad wear and headlight function. The information is relayed to a computer and displayed on a screen. The same computer can also make calculations and display other information, such as fuel consumption and estimated time of arrival. Car designers are now developing cars in which certain vital information, such as road speed, is projected onto a head-up display on the windshield, thus reducing the need for the driver to look away from the road ahead.

Almost every working part of a modern car can now be controlled by a computer. In this Ford concept car, the sunroof closes automatically when a sensor detects moisture in the atmosphere.

In the latest cars the computer is also programmed to process the information and send out instructions to various working parts of the car. This is less easy to achieve than it sounds, as it often requires the use of complex devices that must be triggered by the very small currents used in electronic circuits.

Some electronic control systems have been in use for some time. Electronic fuel injection and electronic ignition were first used in racing and high-performance cars over 20 years ago. Today, they are rapidly becoming standard equipment on ordinary cars, and form the basis of engine management systems. The computer memory stores information about the correct settings of fuel mixture and spark timing for a wide range of speeds and engine loads. The processor uses this information, together with information from the engine sensors, to make constant adjustments to the fuel setting and the ignition timing. This technology results in fuel saving and engine efficiency, and there is less wear and tear on the engine.

Above A computer such as this one is now a vital part of many modern cars. It is the central unit controlling the engine management system.

Below Several makes of cars provide computer information on the instrument panel. The visual displays show fuel consumption, average speed and engine performance.

The Jaguar XJ 220, with a top speed of 220 mph (352 kph), went into production in 1989. The price for this beautiful sports car may well exceed $400,000. It has taken a team of twelve three years to design and perfect this advanced technology sports car.

Electronic control is also being used to make cars safer. Anti-lock brakes reduce the chance of skidding when the brakes are applied. An electronic anti-slip control system acts in the opposite way to stop wheelspin. Microprocessor technology is also being applied to the suspension system of a car, producing what is known as active suspension. Sensors detect movements due to bumps in the road, acceleration, braking and changes in the angle of the body. A microprocessor controls hydraulic pistons in a fluid-filled suspension system to provide a smooth ride and maintain a good grip on the road.

Below A testing sequence for monitoring the performance of anti-lock brakes.

Almost anything can be controlled by a computer, and manufacturers are gradually working toward the fully computerized car. Already there are computer-controlled automatic transmission systems, which at the touch of a button can be set either for speed and power or for economy driving, according to the driver's needs. Some of the latest car designs for the future have "drive-by-wire" systems. Instead of being linked directly to the engine, the accelerator pedal is connected to a computer. The computer also forms the only link between the steering wheel and the front wheels. Some cars already have four-wheel steering, which enables them to be steered around corners more safely.

The ultimate computerized car will be a robot car that automatically drives itself to a programmed destination. Such a car will have to have a system of sensors and microprocessors to keep it on the road and to prevent it from colliding with other road vehicles. Already the technology exists to produce radar or laser systems that would achieve this, although they would be expensive to introduce.

In order for a robot car to find its way, it will need some sort of navigation system and already several kinds of systems have been designed. One system, inertial navigation, would use sensors in the car to detect exactly how far and in what direction the car had moved. Another system could use satellite navigation, originally developed for use by ships and aircraft. Radio signals from any four of a system of eighteen satellites would pinpoint the position of a car on the ground to within thirty feet. The car's navigation computer would then use the information from the sensors or satellites to locate the car's position on a "map" stored on magnetic tape or laser disk. The result would be displayed on a screen inside the car.

Below The Activa was presented to the public in 1988 as Citroen's concept car of the future. This car has a full range of computer-backed features, including "drive-by-wire" steering on all four wheels. The car raises itself, if the doors or hatch are opened, to allow easy access. There are no outside rear-view mirrors. This and the car's wedge shape gives added safety to pedestrians.

The cars of the future are being designed today. Leading car manufacturers compete keenly for their share of the world's car markets, and therefore feel the need to be seen to be at the forefront of today's technological advances. Several manufacturers have now designed and built their own "concept" cars, advanced prototypes or sample cars, that may never actually be produced for the road.

These concept cars provide us with the manufacturers' view of what future cars will be like. Safety, comfort and convenience are featured, with particular emphasis on microprocessor control. Such things as four-wheel steering, active suspension, anti-lock brakes and permanently engaged four-wheel drive will make future cars safer and easier to drive. Other ideas include gearboxes that can be electronically switched from automatic to manual, and rearward-pointing television cameras instead of outside mirrors.

Manufacturers are also conscious of the need to reduce the drag factor of cars still further. Computer-aided design and the use of

wind tunnels can help the development of designs on which even the outside mirrors produce no extra drag.

Car body materials may also change, and future cars may be built using very tough plastics or carbon fiber composites. With these non-rusting materials, cars will last longer.

Improvements are also being made in engines and computerized engine management systems. Ceramic materials are likely to be used increasingly in engines, and new fuels may in time replace those derived from crude oil. Together, all these improvements will ensure that future cars use less fuel and produce less pollution. At the same time they will almost certainly be able to travel faster. Already there are prototypes that can reach speeds of over 200 mph (320 kph). Automobile safety is therefore likely to become even more important.

However, fuel costs, pollution and safety are not the only problems. In many industrialized countries, roads are becoming increasingly congested with traffic, particularly in cities. The problem is not necessarily solved just by improving the roads; experience has shown that this often leads to even more traffic. Outside cities several measures could be used to ease the situation, including the development of automated electronic traffic systems, with constantly updated route guidance for drivers. In cities, however, the car as we know it may disappear. Instead, each city may have limited numbers of driverless robot cabs that will form part of a carefully planned public transportation system. Such changes are unlikely to take place within the next twenty years.

Glossary

Camshaft. Rotating shaft equipped with offset projections, or cams, that operate the valves.

Carburetor. Device operated by engine suction for vaporizing gasoline and mixing the vapor with the correct amount of air for complete combustion.

Ceramic. Tough, clay-like material based on silica (silicon dioxide) combined with elements such as aluminum and magnesium. Ceramics are resistant to high temperatures, shock, abrasion (wear caused by rubbing) and chemicals. They do not conduct heat or electricity and expand very little when heated.

Chassis. A rigid frame used in some cars to support the body and mechanical parts.

Clutch. A device for disconnecting the engine from the gearbox. In a pedal-operated mechanical clutch, a clutch plate is held by springs onto a rotating flywheel on the crankshaft or driveshaft. Depressing the clutch pedal causes the clutch plate to be lifted free of the flywheel.

Coil. The part of the ignition system in which low-voltage current from the battery is converted into high-voltage current that can be used for spark production.

Combustion. The process of burning, in which a substance combines with oxygen, producing heat and flames.

Crankshaft. A shaft carrying offset crankpins. In an internal combustion engine the up and down movement of the pistons is transferred to piston rods. These are connected to the crankpins, and the up and down movement is converted into rotary movement of the crankshaft.

Cylinder. Tube-shaped chamber in which a piston travels back and forth.

Distributor. The part of the ignition system that transmits high-voltage current to the spark plug in the cylinders. A moving rotor arm, driven by the engine at half the crankshaft speed, delivers current to each spark plug in turn. The distributor also contains the make-and-break contacts that the current from the battery to the coil on and off in order to generate a high voltage between the coil and distributor.

Energy. The capacity to do work, such as making something move or heating something up. Energy comes in a variety of forms, which can often be converted from one to another. Thus in a car, chemical energy in fuel is converted into heat energy, which in turn is converted into kinetic (moving) energy in the engine crankshaft. This kinetic energy is transmitted to the road wheels.

Final drive. A system of gears that forms part of the transmission system between the gearbox and the wheels. It contains a system known as the differential, which allows the driven wheels to rotate at different speeds when the car turns a corner.

Flat engine. An engine in which the cylinders lie in two horizontal banks, with the crankshaft between them. The two sets of pistons are thus horizontally opposed.

Gear. A toothed wheel used for transmitting movement from one rotating shaft to another. Gears are usually used to change the speed of rotation.

Gearbox. The part of the transmission system that contains the gears needed to operate the car at different speeds, and in reverse.

Greenhouse effect. The warming of the earth's atmosphere due to increasing amounts of carbon dioxide and other gases.

Half shaft. One of the shafts that links the final drive to the driven road wheels.

Head-up display. A system in which computer information is projected onto the windshield in front of the driver.

Hydraulic. Operated by the pressure of a fluid in a pipe or cylinder.

Hydrocarbon. Chemical whose molecules are made up of hydrogen and carbon only. Such chemicals include methane, propane and the chemicals found in crude oil and its derivatives.

Ignition system. The part of the electrical system used to ignite the fuel in the cylinders of an automobile engine.

Inertial navigation. A system of locating the position of a vehicle by calculating the distance and direction traveled from a known starting point. In a car this can be done relatively easily using sensors in the steering system and wheels to detect changes of direction and the distance covered by the wheels between each change.

Internal combustion engine. An engine in which fuel burns inside a cylinder to drive a piston. The engine may have one or more cylinders.

Laminated. Made up of more than one layer. Modern laminated glass is made up of two layers of glass firmly bonded to a middle layer of tough plastic.

Leaf-spring. A type of spring made up of several long strips of steel (the leaves), each strip being longer than the one below it.

Lubricate. To apply oil to the moving parts of a machine so that they will run freely.

Methane. A hydrocarbon gas, whose molecules consist of one atom of carbon linked to four hydrogen atoms. Methane makes up a large proportion of natural gas.

Microprocessor. A single integrated circuit, or silicon chip, that performs all the functions of the central processing unit of a computer.

Performance. The capabilities of a car, for example, such things as its acceleration, top speed, braking and cornering ability.

Piston. A cylindrical piece of metal, designed to move easily within a cylinder. Piston rings around the outside of the piston ensure a tight seal, and the piston is connected to the crankshaft by a connecting rod.

Pollution. The contamination of the environment by harmful substances.

Propane. A hydrocarbon gas whose molecules contain three carbon atoms and eight hydrogen atoms. Propane is also known as liquefied petroleum gas (LPG) and is produced as a by-product of refining crude oil. It is also obtained directly from natural gas.

Propeller shaft. The shaft that connects the gearbox to the final drive in a rear-wheel-drive car.

Prototype. The original, or model on which something is based.

Rotary engine. An engine in which combustion is converted directly into rotary movement of a driveshaft and some or all of the other moving parts.

Servo mechanism. A control system or motor in which a small input power results in a large output power.

Shock absorber. A device for absorbing some of the energy imparted by sudden shocks..

Spoiler. An aerodynamic device designed to reduce lift on a car and thus hold it down firmly on the road surface.

Sub-frame. A partial chassis, used to support either the front or rear axle of a car.

Suspension. A system of springs and shock absorbers designed to absorb road shocks and provide the occupants of the car with a comfortable ride.

Throttle. A valve that controls the amount of fuel entering an internal combustion engine.

Torsion bar. A round or flat metal rod sometimes used instead of a spring in a suspension system. The bar is subjected to a twisting action, which is resisted by its natural tendency to resume its normal position – just like a coil spring, A torsion bar may also be used as an anti-roll bar, between independent suspension units on opposite sides.

Transmission. The system used to carry the drive power from the engine to the road wheels. It consists of the gearbox, propeller shaft (in rear-wheel-drive cars), final drive and half shafts.

V-engine. An engine in which half the cylinders are arranged at an angle to the other half.

Further reading

Automobile by Daniel Ward (Franklin Watts, 1985)
Automobiles, Rev. Edn. by Jeanne Bendick
(Franklin Watts, 1984)

Super Car by Mike Trier (Gloucester Press, 1988)
Transportation in the Future by Mark Lambert
(Bookwright 1986)

Picture Acknowledgments

The publishers would like to thank the following for allowing their photographs to be reproduced
in this book: BBC Hulton Picture Library 4 (right), 8, 17, 18, 28, 30, 32; Fast Lane Magazine front
cover; The Ford Motor Company 10, 13 (left), 13 (right), 14, 19, 24, 26, 27 (below), 38, 39 (above);
Haymarket Motoring Photo Library 40 (below); Porsche Cars Great Britain Limited 20, 27
(above), 31 (above), 31 (below), 33 (above); Rex Features Limited – photographs by Nils
Jorgensen 21 (above), 21 (below); Spectrum Colour Library 13 (above), 37 (above), 37 (below),
39 – photograph by Keith Jones; Topham 23, 35, 40 (above), 41; ZEFA 4 (left), 5, 22, 25, 29, 33
(below). Artwork by the Hayward Art Group, except for pages 42 and 43 by Nick Hawken.

Index